Nathaniel Brassey Halhed

A Letter to the Rt. Hon. Edmund Burke

On the Subject of his late Charges against the Governor-General of Bengal

Nathaniel Brassey Halhed

A Letter to the Rt. Hon. Edmund Burke
On the Subject of his late Charges against the Governor-General of Bengal

ISBN/EAN: 9783337106782

Printed in Europe, USA, Canada, Australia, Japan

Cover: Foto ©ninafisch / pixelio.de

More available books at **www.hansebooks.com**

A
LETTER

TO THE

Rt. Hon. EDMUND BURKE,

ON THE SUBJECT OF

HIS LATE CHARGES

AGAINST THE

GOVERNOR-GENERAL

OF

BENGAL:

LONDON:

Printed by J. JOHNSON, (No. 232) WHITECHAPEL,

MDCCLXXXIII.

A

LETTER, &c.

RIGHT HONOURABLE SIR,

I CANNOT but condole with you on the unwelcome publication of Mr. Haftings's late Letter to the Court of Directors; not merely becaufe the honour which, as a moft able compofition, it reflects upon the talents of its Author, muft naturally be grating to an enmity fo rancorous and implacable as Your's; but (what is infinitely more mortifying) becaufe the confcious warmth of innocence, the irrefiftable force of truth, and the

A 2   naked

naked display of fact, with which every line of it is replete, have at once confuted, over-turned and done away the whole of those frivolous, indecent, and unsupported charges, which for two Years together have been obtruded on the public, from the Select Committee. I say *the whole*, altho' that wonderful letter comprehends a compleat summary only of the grounds and circumstances of the revolution at Benares. But as the expulsion of Cheyt Sing was your strong ground, and as your remarks have been particularly intemperate and acrimonious on that subject; a candid, ample, and satisfactory exculpation from all your criminatory discussions on this one article, secures an unprejudiced hearing, and, (as you will one day feel,) a thorough acquittal in all the rest.——

This revolution at Benares appears indeed to have occupied an exclusive share of your attention. From the first moment that imperfect intelligence of the transaction arrived, you fastened on it with an eagerness that exhibited nothing less than impartiality: and precipitately hurried the crude materials into the House of Commons in your second

Report,

Report, before it was poffible, that any clear
or liberal judgment could be formed of the
merits of the affair. As foon, however, as
the uncertainty of vague furmife had given
place to fomewhat of confiftent information,
Governor Johnftone, in one of the moft powerful pieces of oratory that ever dignified a
popular Affembly, turned the tide of opinion
decidedly againft you, and eftablifhed the
prudence, the juftice, the policy of the
Governor General's conduct, on grounds
which temerity itfelf, urged by all the impulfe of malevolence, would hardly have attempted to undermine. But Your purpofes
are not fo eafily fhaken; Your verfatility is
not fo fpeedily foiled; and I can readily difcover in your late Supplement to the fecond
Report (which indeed you may well blufh
not to have been the firft fyllable you have
uttered on that topic) as many objections
aimed at the Governor's admirable Speech, as
at the Narrative of Mr. Haftings, which for
the firft time you have now had the opportunity to difcufs, and whom you had pre-
vioufly vilified, reprobated, and condemned
with half his ftory untold. — Here too your
triumph is miferably interrupted, by the un-
feafonable

feafonable arrival of the Governor General's moft excellent Letter,—addrefled indeed, to the Court of Directors, but more immediately applicable to You : For They, to fay the truth, have been but too much the humble inftrument of your paffions, and their dictates feem but Echoes to the Reports of the Select Committee.——You have, Sir, been fingularly induftrious in precluding from the Councils of Leadenhall-Street, every poffible chance or pretenfion to originality, in the Condemnation of any of Mr. Haftings's public meafures : And I have now before me in the Contents of your ninth and tenth Reports, and in your Supplement to the fecond, anticipated abufe, and prompted Anathemas on almoft every fubject, which is likely to be agitated in the Court of Directors, as matter for their general Letters to Bengal in the approaching feafon. The opinions, the politics, the commands of the Eaft-India Company originate in the Select Committee Chamber, and *their* correfpondence is become little more than the vehicle of Mr. Burke's fpeculative incoherencies and injurious perfonalities. It is not therefore more extraordinary, that Mr. Haftings's late Letter, containing a complete

, refutation

refutation of certain articles alledged and maintained by the Court of Directors, should still more pointedly meet the topics on which you have since so unmercifully insisted : than that the same objections started many months ago by the Directors, should at a subsequent period occupy a distinguished place in one of Your Reports, amplified, embellished, and improved with all your fertility of invention and artifice of arrangement. In compliment to the reluctance with which I know you must quit Cheyt Sing's cause, and to gratify your ears once more with the pleasing sound of that favourite name, I shall in the course of my correspondence, take the liberty of adding a few observations, however superfluous, to the manly, victorious, and conclusive arguments of the Governor General. And though in the present state of things, humbled, (as you must be) by the consciousness of detection in premeditated untruths ; debased (as you most assuredly are) in the eyes of the public, as much for the gross illiberality of your attacks on some of the brighteſt characters of the age, as for Your unblushing patronage of convicted defaulters ; and consigned (as you will very soon experience)

ence) to the scorn and neglect of those very colleagues, whose purposes your duplicity had served, or whose sympathy your necessities had excited, there can be little probability, that the poison you have already administered, should ever work its malignant operation, and still less that you should hereafter be suffered to litter the Speaker's table with a fresh dose : I cannot let your unprecedented malice shelter itself under the obscurity of public indifference, without once more casting down the gauntlet of defiance to all your attempts for affixing the slightest stigma of delinquency on the character of Mr, Hastings. I have already, Sir, with all humility attended your progress through eight voluminous Reports : I narrowly scrutinized their several contents, and have imparted the result of my observations to the public. I have yet to learn, that any thing false, or injurious, or uncandid, has fallen from my pen : my tale has been plain and unvarnished, but it has not been denied, and it cannot be confuted. I now enter the lists with confidence. The world is apprized of the side on which truth has hitherto combated, and the half of your assertions is already

ready

ready difbelieved before I write a fyllable: the reft are fufpected for their mere plaufibility. Mr. Burke is no longer a formidable opponent; obftinately induftrious in the ruin of a man whom he cannot imitate, he lofes his temper in proportion as the tafk becomes more difficult: and endeavours by the fcurrility of his language to make up for the deficiency of his reafonings. A Fencing mafter in a paffion is difarmed by the meaneft of his Scholars: and I am not the only antagonift who has taken advantage of your very fury to aim, a fuccefsful attack. You have read the Letters of *a Citizen* in the Morning Herald—You have feen two Letters from Major Scott, on the infinuations contained in the ninth Report: Should your doughty Chairman be ever permitted or induced to ftagger to the Speaker's Chair with another Ream of fophiftical abfurdities, half the town will ftart up to diffect and expofe them. Every man who can hold a pen, will employ it in the detection of fome frefh error or untruth, and your Reports will excite a difguft and difrefpect as general as that which hath of late notorioufly attended your fpeeches.

B.   After

After all, can you suppose that the public, eager to testify their exalted sense of Mr. Hastings's political merits, and to taste their immediate advantages, will stoop to dabble in the miserable dirt of your 9th Report? Can you flatter yourself, that the stale and wretched dregs of Mr. Francis's criminatory manufactory, still retain venom enough to hurt the Governor-General? For the despicable insipidity of such a second-hand potion silent contempt is the proper antidote. But that you may not find one source of triumph even in the escape from palpable detection, I will here hastily answer the most virulent of the charges brought forward in your 9th Report, under their several heads.

1st. Nundcomar's execution.

You write (Ninth Report, page 7.) " The " sufferer, the Rajah Nundcomar, appears " at the very time of this extraordinary pro- " secution, a discoverer of some particulars " of illicit gain, then charged upon Mr. " Hastings, the Governor General."——

Major

Major Scott has informed you with truth, that Mr. Haftings neither did, nor could interfere in the Trial or Execution of Nundcomar : and I now add, that the Raja was *no difccverer*, (for he could never fubftantiate a fingle difcovery) but a lying informer; that in his laft moments, he thought of nothing lefs than of making good his affertions refpecting the Governor General's peculations, and that the paper written the night before his execution, which was afterwards burnt as a libel, did not contain a fyllable relative to that fubject. A perfon who tranflated that paper, from the Raja's own writing, is ready to fwear to the fact.

2d. New Plan of Remittance, Page 19.

The Company's exiftence in Europe is founded on commerce; and their Sales at the India-Houfe are the only means of keeping up the neceffary circulation of cafh. It is poffible that the Company *might* fubfift, and it is fair to fuppofe it fully equal to the trial of fubfifting for one year without any actual gain whatfoever: but without circulation it is impoffible that it fhould fubfift at all. The

Bengal

Bengal government finding it impracticable to convert any part of their current revenues into goods for Europe, and being therefore unable to fecure to the Company its cuftomary profits, were obliged, as their laft refcurce, to advert to a plan for enfuring, at leaft, the cir- culation of cafh. For however the Committee may be inclined to doubt the fact, it is moft certain, that " fuch a fcheme" (as that origi- nally propofed by the Council-general, or *any* fcheme) " is preferable to the *total fufpenfion* " *of trade*,"—which in my opinion implies neither more nor lefs than *inftant bankruptcy*. When the firft outline of the plan arrived, the Select Committee, with their ufual alacrity, went to work upon the difcovery and difplay of its every probable or poffible difadvantage : and had, it appears, proceeded fo far as to leave it dubious *(to themfelves only,)* whether it would not have been almoft as convenient to have fufpended the trade entirely ; when another difpatch brought word that the firft plan had been fet afide altogether ; and that the Council-General had found the means of negociating a loan for the provifion of the current inveftment (notwithftanding all their diftreffes and difficulties) at a rate nearly as

favour-

favourable (and much more fo in refpect to the *time* at which the drafts are to be given) as that which to the Dutch, Danes, and Portugueze, has been for fome years paft the main fpring of all their Indian commerce. Candour furely required that objections to a fcheme which *had not taken place*, fhould have been fuppreffed ; at leaft that its *defects* fhould have been contrafted with the comparative *merits* of the new one. So far from it, that the Committee having laboured with all their fophiftical acrimony, to deny and condemn the original fcheme, gravely inform us, (when their bile is exhaufted) that *no fuch fcheme exifts:* and then proceed with the fame impartiality of ftatement, and delicacy of obfervation, to comment on *that* which has been fubftituted in its place. " The fituation of the " Company," they obferve (Page 22) " under " this perpetual variation of fyftem in their " inveftment, is truly perplexing." Granted. But this perplexity is an evil inherent in the very core and conftitution of commerce. And indeed I am much furprized, that neither Mr. Burke, nor any of his refpectable friends, fhould have known, or heard, or furmifed, that in all fituations, a neceffity of borrowing

money

money fubjects the borrower to a thoufand perplexities in the mode, and that even the credit of the Britifh nation will not enable a Minifter to dictate the terms of his loan.

3d. Opium Contract given to Mr. Sulivan.

After much mifreprefentation and falfe reafoning on the fubject of this Contract, all of which Major Scott has fatisfactorily refuted, you fay, Page 39, " Your Committee ex-
" amining Mr. Higginfon, late a Member of
" the Board of Trade on that fubject, were
" informed, that this Contract, very foon after
" the making, *was generally underftood* at Cal-
" cutta, to have been fold to this Mr. Benn—
" but that he could not *particularize the fum*
" for which it had been affigned ; and that
" Mr. Benn had afterwards fold it to Mr.
" Young." You then, in the true fpirit of Committee-inference, *pronounce upon the fact :*
" By this *tranfaction* it *appears clearly*, that the
" Contract was given to Mr. Sulivan for no
" other purpofe than to fupply him with a
" fum of money." What *tranfaction* do you mean, and where does any thing *appear fo clearly ?* Mr. Higginfon ftates a general re-

port,

port, of which he does not pretend to afcer-tain the circumftances, and with you it is in a moment transformed, by hocus pocus, into a *tranfaction*. Surely fuch a dealer in vernacular literature as yourfelf muft have recollected, that, " one fhould never believe above half " of a Report." (even fetting thofe of the Se-lect Committee out of the queftion.) Poffibly, Sir, upon fecond enquiry, you might find the whole tranfaction to exift only in the Report, of which *your* Report is the echo, and that Mr. Sulivan holds the contract *for himfelf* to this day.

4th. Colonel M'Lean's offer of refignation in the name of Mr. Haftings.

In the 52d page of the Ninth Report, you have condefcended to make ufe of this pitiful ftory ; and you remark on it, that " a fanction " was hereby given to all future defiance of " every authority in this kingdom." You forget, that *twice* fince that period, the firft Minifter of this country has effectually an-nulled the whole tranfaction by a parliamen-tary re-appointment of Mr. Haftings ; and that even fuppofing the refignation at that time

time valid (which his Majefty's Judges in India denied, and which neither the Directors, nor the King's Minifters, nor you, with all your logic, have attempted to eftablifh *upon proof*) Mr. Haftings, under the two fubfequent acts of parliament, is altogether a new Governor-General, and acts under a new commiffion, totally independent of the former.

5th. Difobedience of Orders, page 54, &c.

The Houfe of Commons, the Miniftry, the whole nation, are equally fick of your nau-feous tautology, and incorrigible mifreprefentations, refpecting the removal of Meffrs. Briftow and Fowke, from their offices. Major Scott, both in his evidence before your Committee, and in his printed letter to you, has explained the merits of their removal in the moft explicit terms. The neceffity of political confidence between the principal and fubordinates in the adminiftration of a kingdom, and in the intercourfe between different nations, is furely as apparent, as *that* of a *good underftanding* between the head of an office and his clerks. And then that *You*, Sir, of all others, fhould fo long and fo loudly exclaim

againft

against such sort of exertions !—But I beg your pardon.—When you Ninth Report was fabricated, you might flatter yourself that the gauze of hypocrisy which had so repeatedly succeeded in concealing the real designs of Mr. Burke, would prove ample enough to cloak, and substantial enough to hide the mysteries of Messrs. Powel and Bembridge. Mr. Hastings removed Messrs. Bristow and Fowke, to make room for others whom he could trust, and *without whom he could not execute to advantage the business of his station.* You are, perhaps, by this time, convinced that he was right.

6th. Removal of Mahomed Reza Khan, Page 58, &c.

If you will take the trouble to turn to page 22 of your 5th Report, you will find the majority of the Council-General at Calcutta, to have " Resolved, that the Board recommend " Mahomed Reza Khan, to the Nabob, to be " Minister of the Government, and *guardian* " *of his minority.*" Upon this appointment the Directors express their sentiments, Page 24, as follows, " We were always of opinion,

C " that

" that an able, oftenfible Minifter, *during the*
" *minority of the Nabob*, would be neceflary."
Is it not clear by implication, that the Council-General alluded to, and the Directors underftood, the probability of a change in
this appointment, when the Nabob's minority. fhould be expired ? Mahomed Reza
Khan's behaviour appears to have been uniformly difgufting to the Nabob; and the
leaft furely that the lineal defcendant of
the acknowledged Sovereign of the country (himfelf alfo titular fovereign) could
claim, was an exemption from the interference
of a man whom he detefted, in his private
affairs : from the domeftic tyranny of a native,
certainly his inferior, and nominally his fubject.—If his inexperience rendered fome controul neceffary, that controul muft be much
lefs galling, if exerted through the immediate
influence of the actual government, and by
one of thofe Foreigners, whofe perfonal and
unqueftioned fuperiority had acquired them
the decided dominion of the whole country.

I now come to your favorite fubject, *the*
revolution of Benares, wherein you observe

(1ft

(1ft page, fupplement to 2d report) that
" Cheyt Sing, fon and fucceffor to Bulwant
" Sing,—was deprived of all rank, power and
" command in that Zemindarry, *which was*
" *the inheritance of his anceftors*." How you
came by this *tail-piece* of your information, I
will not prefume to afk; for although I am
fure that Cheyt Sing himfelf did *not*, in fact,
fucceed to the Zemindarry by any legal and
authentic *title of inheritance*; his anceftors, for
ought I know, might have held and availed
themfelves of fuch a claim fome generations
back, and you may have been exclufively fa-
voured with a view of the *title deeds*. This
circumftance, however, of the *inheritance*, was
providently inferted to fecure a more ready
affent to your remark, fubfequently intro-
duced (page 5) " Your Committee do not
" find the Governor-General well founded in
" his affertion, that it was from *his influence*
" that Cheyt Sing obtained the *firft legal* title
" that his family ever poffeffed, of property
" in the land, in 1773," &c. &c. This objection, which coft you near two pages to
difcufs (altho' you grant it be nothing to the
purpofe, but to fhew that no objection comes
amifs) refts fimply upon " *inconteftible proof*,"

which

(which I shall not difpute with you) " that
" Rajah Cheyt Sing had *actually enjoyed all the*
" *rights of a Zemindar* three years before that
" period."—But you ought to have proved
that Cheyt Sing *then*, or at *any time before*,
poffeffed a *legal title* to thofe rights. Mr.
Haftings's affection goes only to the *acquifi-
tion of the title*, not to the *enjoyment of the
rights*; I hofe had been held by interpofition,
by conn,vance, by ufurpation,— by what you
will,—*but not by a legal title*. Let me afk you,
Sir, what you underftand by " *a Zemindarry?*" is it not an hereditary Fief ? is it not
the neceffary inherent property of a Zemindarry
to be *hereditary*; and is it not in proof that
Cheyt Sing did *not* come to it by *inheritance?*
You well know (for it is to be found in the
10th and 11th pages of your 2d Report) that
when Rajah Bulwant Sing died, the Government of Bengal informed the Court of Directors, " of the confequence it was to their
" affairs, that the fucceffion to the Zemin-
" darry of Benares fhould continue in the
" family, but *that it was a delicate point to ac-
" complifh with the Vizier*,—that the occafion
" demanded immediate difpatch, and the Pre-
" fident was requefted to write to the Vizier
" accordingly,

" accordingly, *in favor of the son of the late*
" *Rajah*, in terms that would least awake
" his jealousy.—A jealous, suspicious dis-
" position of the old Rajah—may possibly
" have been the reason why the son *was not*
" *included* in the treaty of 1765, for had he ex-
" pressed *a wish to secure the Zemindarry in his*
" *own family*, at a time when the Vizier was
" receiving back his Country from our hands,
" a doubt can scarcely be formed but it
" would have been attended with success:
" but suspicious probably of the conse-
" quences that *his son should think he had a*
" *right to the succession*,—his whole aim seem'd
" to center in self-security." The Vizier, it
clearly appears, had given Bulwant Sing a
Cowlnama *for himself only*: the treaty of Alla-
habad expressed no more (2d Report, page
16.) Cheyt Sing was admitted (" *at the earnest*
" *recommendation and request*" of the Bengal-
Council (page 11) and *not* upon any *legal title*
or claim *of right* whatsoever) to hold the Zemindarry *on the same terms as his Father*, (i. e.
in capite.) At this time therefore the tenure
was at least *precarious*: the Vizier " con-
" sidered his former act as of little validity,"
(page 12) and the Council of Bengal must
have

have had some suspicions of the same nature, by impowering Mr. Hastings to " *renew the* " *stipulation*" (page 11). The Governor accordingly, to remove all ambiguity, changed the very essence of the tenure, by obtaining from the Vizier an engagement, " confirm-" ing to Rajah Cheyt Sing *and his posterity*, " the stipulations formerly made in behalf of " his father, Bulwant Sing."—This therefore establishes beyond a possibility of cavil, what the Governor General asserts in his narrative : " Cheyt Sing obtained from our influ-" ence, *exerted by myself*, the *first legal title* that " his family ever possessed of *property in the* " *land*, (mark that) of which he, till then, " was only the Aumil, and of which he be-" came the acknowledged *Zemindar*, by a sun-" nud granted to him by the Nabob, Sujah " Dowlah, *at my instance*, in the month of " September, 1773. Mr. Hastings therefore, even in this preliminary article (which you have gone out of your way to overset,) in this assertion, " which appeared quite contra-" dictory to the matter contained in their " (the Committee's) former Report," is, as usual, manifestly in the right, and you are in the wrong. And now having disincumbered

Cheyt

Cheyt Sing of the *inheritance of his anceſtors*, I
will, with your leave, proceed to examine
thoſe *rights*, which, whether as Aumil, Tributary Zemindar, or *Prince and Noble of the
Country*, you are ſo anxious to inveſt him
with. Your mode of aſcertaining theſe rights
is peculiar to the ſyſtem adopted for the general uſe of your India Reports. It conſiſts *not*
in quoting the different articles of the deed,
by which he holds the Zemindarry from the
Company: but in garbling from different mi-
nutes of the different Members of the Council
General at different periods, their different
opinions as to *what indulgence* it would be po-
litically uſeful and proper to allow the Raja,
as his general rights. That the Gentlemen of
the Council ſhould thus ſettle among them-
ſelves (Supplement to 2d Report, pages 13
and 14) what ſort of privileges they would
be pleaſed to admit for his rights, amounts
in my mind to a proof, that in point of
legal title or eſtabliſhed pretenſion, he poſ-
ſeſſed no rights but ſuch as were common to
other ſubjects of the Mogul Empire. The
ſeparate opinions delivered in the Council-
General, which are ſo often invidiouſly quoted through your Supplement, are by no
means

means binding on the Company at large on any other principle, than as they became the grounds of thole public inftruments. by which Cheyt Sing held his Territory. It would be very amufing, if all the difcordant fentiments uttered in his Majefty's Cabinet, were to be appealed to as rules of State, or ties upon Government. I cannot however quit thefe opinions of Council, without a fhort tribute of applaufe to Mr. Barwell's accurate experience of Afiatic te.npers, and well-told prognoftication of Cheyt Sing's defection, fix years before it happened.—" The Rajah fhould " have the ftrongeft tie of intereft to fupport " our Goveramnt, in cafe of any future rup- " ture with the Soubah of Oude. To make " this his intereft, he muft not be tributary " to the Englifh Government; for from the " inftant he becomes its tributary, from that " moment we may expect him to fide againft " us, and *by taking advantage of the troubles* " *and commctions that may arife, attempt to difbur-* " *den himfelf of his pecuniary obligations.*" (Supplement, page 13.) The Governor-General had uniformly recommended favourable terms for Cheyt Sing, under the idea, (Page 12) that, " by proper encouragement and pro-
" tection

" tection he may prove a profitable depen-
" dent, an useful barrier, and even a *powerful*
" *ally* to the Company." But these favourable terms never could become *rights*, unless
ratified by the Sunnud and Cabooleat, which
united the two parties: And a man who
could refuse to contribute 5 lacks of rupees
out of 30, and to furnish 1000 cavalry out of
above 1700 (see Appendix) to the relief of
his Sovereign's most pressing exigencies, certainly proved himself a most disaffected subject, and but little qualified for an useful
ally. If Mr. Hastings, in 1773, " resisted an
" application, made in very earnest terms by
" the Vizier, to dispossess Cheyt Sing' of his
" forts of Bidjegur and Luttyfpoor," (page
15) it was not so much on account of the
Raja's independent right to them, as for the
purpose of securing to the Company a Barrier against that very Vizier,—a measure
which was always uppermost in his thoughts:
and though it be true, that in 1775, it was
the Governor-General's opinion (page 14)
" that the perpetual and independent pos-
" session of the Zemindarry of Benares, and
" its dependencies, should be *confirmed and*
" *guaranteed* to Cheyt Sing, and his heirs for
D " ever"—

" ever"—it is no lefs in proof, that "the
" Governor-General's propofitions did *not* ex-
" clufively form the bafis of the treaty
" with Afoph-ul-Dowla;" and therefore this
opinion, that Cheyt Sing *ought* to have been
totally freed from the *remains* of his then *vaffalage*, cannot operate againft his conduct,
under an agreement different from that propofed by him, and upon a fyftem, which only
transferred thofe "*remains of vaffalage*," whatever they might be, by which Cheyt Sing
was then bound, from one Sovereign to another. Admitting, however, *all* the *fpeculative
rights*, with which the Select Committee have
been pleafed to inveft Cheyt Sing, I do not
find among them, even by implication, the
right of defending himfelf by the fword againft
his *lawful Sovereign*. That at leaft is a right
not compatible with the principles of Afiatic
Government; and the Committee's miferable
fubterfuge in his apology, does but little ho-
nor either to their logic or their politics.
" The Rajah's conduct on this trying and
" tempting occafion (fupplement, page 18)
" does not appear to have been that of an
" enterprizing Chief, impatient under the ex-
" ercife of any kind of fuperiority over him,
" and

" and therefore refolved to aim at indepen-
" dence, whenever the means of attainment
" were in his power ; *on the contrary*, his ob-
" ject was to efcape from confinement, and
" then to fly to his forts *for the fecurity of his*
" *perfon.*" Has the Governor-General ever
difplayed fo fanguinary a difpofition ? or was
there within the limits of conjecture any
caufe, that Cheyt Sing fhould be apprehen-
five for the fecurity of his perfon ? It was his
perfon that Mr. Haftings meant to *fecure*, and
thought he had fecured, by the arreft : and
would the Committee now infinuate it as their
opinion, that this very arreft gave Cheyt
Sing a right to maffacre two companies of
Seapoys with their European Officers ; and
that not on the inftant of furprife and fudden
impulfe of paffion, but on a deliberate paufe,
in the moment of calm reflection, *in cold blood!*
To what offences in your opinion, Sir, would
the *Crimen læfæ Majeftatis* apply ? Had the
legal, the acknowledged Sovereign *no right at*
all, as *Sovereign*, and was no fubmiffion due
from Cheyt Sing, *as a fubject* ? After all, to
what fpecific act of the Governor-General
can Cheyt Sing's conduct be attributed ?
Not to the intended fine, for of that he is

probably

probably ignorant to this hour. Not to the
arreſt, for he had " quietly ſubmitted to that
" arreſt, and ſent a letter to the Governor-
" General, which indicates the moſt perfect
" obedience."—(page 16) So far from having ſubſequently received any cauſe for freſh
alarm, Mr. Haſtings had written to him in
terms expreſsly calculated to encourage him
under his " apparent deſpondency," and the
Rajah had anſwered him, " *I am entirely free*
" *from concern and apprehenſion.*" Yet, on the
ſame day, within a few hours, our troops
were maſſacred, the Rajah *fled to his forts,* the
ſtandard of revolt was ſet up, contagious rebellion ſpread through the whole Country,—
every hand was prepared to arm, and arms
were in readineſs for every hand ; and we are
now told, in the ſhuffling cant of an Old-
Bailey excuſe, that " his *object* was to *eſcape*
" *from confinement.*" The extent, however, of
his military preparations, clearly evince his
predetermined views of reſiſtance, in caſe of
any attack, and by conſtructive evidence
convict him of *treaſon,* even before a ſword
was drawn : His deſperate conduct, in con-
ſequence of a mere exertion of civil power,
effectually

effectually annihilated *all his rights*, and completed the measure of his guilt.

As your Committee have spared no pains, however ill-bestowed, to establish the *independent rights* of Rajah Cheyt Sing, *as a Zemindar*, it would have been no more than decently impartial, had they given themselves the trouble to enquire whether or not the Company, as immediate sovereign of the Zemindarry, did not by the very constitution of the state and the nature of all Mogul tenures, stand possessed also of some *clear, original,* and *inherent rights,* of which it could not by any partial or temporary agreement, be divested, so long as it should continue to be the acknowledged paramount. Of this sort of rights, in my humble opinion, *military service* is the very first. It is indeed most notoriously the grand pervading principle of all feodal governments. In the most flourishing times of the Hindostanic Emperors, even the personal attendance of the great Rajahs and Zemindars was constantly required and exacted both at court and in camp : all the European travellers of the two last centuries, concur in testifying, that the guard of the Emperor's

perfon

person was committed to the dependent Rajahs. The Ayeen-y Acberee (or description of the arrangements of the Mogul empire under Acber) contains as well an enumeration of the forces kept by each Zemindar, as the quantum of tribute in which he was assessed: and it was to this established and uncontrovertible system of the empire, that Mr. Barwell alluded in his minute (2d Report, 27 page) " An acquisition of revenue and *military* " *force*, I suppose to have been annexed to the " grant of the Zemindarry of Benares and " Gauzipore to the Company." He was undoubtedly right; for the transfer of the sovereignty included both. Cheyt Sing maintained a considerable number of troops, and by the feodal tenure of all Zemindarries, was bound to furnish his quota of them, in case of war, to his paramount. But the necessity under which our government lay, of demanding *in money* the amount of this quota, instead of burthening itself with a set of ill-paid and worse-disciplined banditti, has in the present case most unfortunately afforded the means of quibbling on the denomination of the demand, and has transformed *a legal* constitutional requisition of *military service* into an *unjustifiable* exaction

exaction of an *encreased tribute*. And yet the original minute of the Governor-General rested the matter on its proper ground, " That Raja Cheyt Sing be required in form to " contribute his share of the burthen of the " present war, by consenting to the establish- " ment of *three regular battalions of Seapoys*, to " be raised and maintained at his expence." (2d Report, page 26.) To this measure, there could exist upon Mogul principles, only one objection. It *might* have been urged that the demand exceeded the proportion of troops at which the Zemindarry of Benares, &c. stood rated in the books of the empire, or the actual number which it could now furnish. But *that plea* is obviated by our certain know- ledge, that Cheyt Sing's ordinary infantry ex- ceeded the number of *six* battalions : so that when he was required to furnish *three* to his Sovereign, he had nothing to do, but imme- diately reduce the same number at home. This mode of stating the rights and foundations of the transaction, at once shews the jesuitical so- phistry of your observation, (Supplement, page 6.) " Your Committee cannot discover " any record to prove, that although an ex- " traordinary demand of *money*, beyond the sti- " pulated

" pulated rent paid by the Rajah, was made
" in July, that the whole payment of it was
" *confequently* due the moment in which the
" demand was made." That the demand in
queftion was for *money*, is an accident which
does not at all partake of the intrinfic merits of
the affair. —The demand was properly for *foldiers*; the money was merely a commutation
or fubftitute. The foldiers were certainly due
when demanded, becaufe the Sovereign was at
war; fuch being the tenure of the Zemindarry,
confequently the money was due; becaufe the due
quota of troops could not be raifed, nor maintained without it. The war, and of courfe
the occafion for military fervice, had continued for two years, and was advanced into
the third, when the revolution at Benares
took place. From the firft moment to the
laft Cheyt Sing had exerted every artifice of
prevarication, fubterfuge, and falfehood, to
protract, to modify, or to elude the demand.
In the firft year he contrived to delay payment for near three months, (Supplement,
page 6.) In the fecond, no other anfwer could
be procured from him by the Refident, than
" a pofitive affertion that the Rajah *could not*
" pay it." (2d Report, page 34.) At the
end

end of four months, however, when every softer method failed, he was dragooned into compliance. His conduct in the third year was equally perverse; past experience had no effect upon his avaricious obstinacy; and when nearly three months were expired, the Resident wrote to Calcutta, that " the Rajah, " notwithstanding his *solemn assurances*, has hi- " therto paid *no part* of the balance of his sub- " sidy. He has resumed the plea of inability, " *and I can form no opinion how long he may think proper to protract payment*" (Page 46.) On receipt of this letter, the patience even of Mr. Francis and Mr. Wheler was exhausted. They had hitherto opposed all compulsive measures, or even threats ; but now they were roused to a sense of the indignity offered to government, and unanimously voted for the rigorous exaction both of the balance *due* upon his subsidy, and of a fine in punishment of his contumacy. The same arguments that have established the right of government to exact military service from its dependent Ze-mindars, will extend to all cases in which that military service can be applied; *consequently* to the requisition of *cavalry*, as well as of *infantry*. Cheyt Sing's establishment of

the

the former, by his own acknowledgement, a-
mounted to 1300 (2d Report, page 39)
though the Select Committee, in their Supplement (page 11) have reduced the number,
undoubtedly by mistake, to 1200; From
some documents in the Appendix to the Governor General's narrative, there is reason to
suppose he maintained near 2000. The Resident, after various fruitless applications, delivered him a peremptory order to prepare
1000 horse; The Rajah, by his own confession,
collected but 500 at most, and offered 500 bur-
gundosses, (miserable infantry) as a substitute
for the remainder. The Select Committee
observe upon this, " it is somewhat singular,
" that the Governor-General declares in 1775,
" that he did not mean to impose this demand
" of cavalry on the Rajah, by compulsion;
" and yet in 1781, his not complying with
" this demand, is considered as such an act
" of delinquency, as to form one of the two
" direct charges of culpability and guilt; and
" for the pardon of which he was to pay
" largely, or a severe vengeance was to be
" exacted for his delinquency." (Supplement,
page 13.) Never was comparison more unhappy—never were two cases more dissimilar,

than

than thofe here unnaturally claffed together !
In 1775, in time of profound peace, and in
the act of forming an agreement with the
Rajah, Mr. Haftings fhewed an unwillingnefs
to faddle him with the neceffity of conftantly
maintaining 2000 cavalry. General Clavering
however underftood even then, that the Rajah
did " *keep up a large body of Cavalry.*" (Page
12,) and the Council General recommended
to him to keep two thoufand. In 1781,
in the midft of all the exigencies of
war, and under the fanction of that particular
tenure, by which Cheyt Sing then held his
Zemindarry, i. e. the conftitutional obligation of military fervice, Mr. Haftings, as reprefentative of the actual Sovereign, required
of him the affiftance of fuch cavalry as he
then had in his pay, fuppofed, agreeably to
the above quoted recommendation of the
Council General, in 1775, to be 2000. The
demand however was gradually reduced to
1500, and laftly to 1000. The Rajah acknowledged to have in pay 1300 (2d Report,
page 49) yet at moft offered but 500,—and
as the Governor-General ftates in his narrative, (page 7) " *furnifhed none.*"

E 2   Thefe

These instances of contumacy and disobedience appeared in the Governor-General's opinion, " evidences of a deliberate and " systematic conduct, aiming at the total sub- " version of the authority of the Company, " which design had been long and generally " imputed to him," (Supplement, page 17) The Committee, on the contrary, " can con- " ceive these circumstances to have happened " without any design whatever in Cheyt Sing " to give umbrage to the Administration of " Calcutta,".—Nay, they can affert that *" succeeding events have clearly proved it."* And yet, if these circumstances, combined with the deliberate maffacre of two companies, for no oftenfible cause whatever ; with the after-discovery of military ftores, warlike preparations and numerous troops, all kept in profound fecrecy, and for no poffible purpofes of ne- ceffary defence : with the fudden revolt of his whole Country almoft at a fignal, and with the general good underftanding which inftantly appeared between him and all the other difaffected Chiefs in the neighbouring Provinces, do not form a body of evidence fatisfactorily demonftrable of " treachery, " perfidy, and rebellious violence," I know

not

not under what definitions, or by what kind of conftruction, treafon and revolt can poffi- bly have been expreffed in any criminal Code, fince the firft inftitution of political So-cieties. But in the Reports of the Select Committee, infinuation is an arrant Proteus: No fooner have I caught him in one fhape, than in the inftant of conviction he eludes my grafp, and rifes another being in the next page. We are now told, that " unlefs the " depofal of Cheyt Sing, was a meafure *ab-* " *folutely pre-determined,* before the Governor " General proceeded to acts of violence, the " Rajah *might have been informed of the extent* " *of his guilt.*" (Supplement, page 19.) And fo He *was.* Mr. Haftings's firft letter (2d Report, page 48) from Benares, exprefs-ly fays, " The firft ftep, which I judged it " neceffary to take, as the ground on which " my future proceedings were to be conduct- " ed, was to *recapitulate in writing,* the feveral " inftances of his conduct, which for fome " time paft, have repeatedly drawn upon " him the fevere reprehenfions of the board; " and to demand a *clear and fatisfactory ex-* " *planation.*" The anfwer fent by Cheyt Sing to this letter here defcribed, was the

fartheft

fartheft from *clear* or *satisfactory*. It was filled with fhuffling excufes and palpable lies; particularly the Rajah writes (in fpite of his grofs mifconduct in delaying to furnifh military aid) " I complied, *with the utmoft* " *readinefs*, with the order You fent me for " the payment of five lacks of Rupees on " account of the war." (2d Report, page 49.) Mr. Haftings obferved upon the whole of this anfwer, that it was " not only un- " fatisfactory in fubftance, but offenfive in " ftyle, and lefs a vindication of himfelf, " than a recrimination upon me." (page 50) Alarmed at thefe appearances, fo different from the conduct of an Indian fubject to his acknowledged fovereign, the Governor Ge- neral, hefitating between the *neceffity* of affert- ing the authority of that Government, of which He was reprefentative, and the alarm which the full exertion even of juftifiable feverity might occafion at fo critical a period— took the mild medium of an arreft. There is no clue whatever for the fuppofition that this very arreft, much lefs that the *depofal* of Cheyt Sing was " *a meafure abfolutely predeter-* " *mined,*" or even thought of, till his contu- macious reply to the Governor-General's ex- poftupostulation rendered some effort of rigour clearly indispensable. If the arrest were (and it cannot be doubted) an act growing out of unforeseen emergencies, what followed were events totally out of the Governor-General's option or controul. His prisoner fled, his troops murdered, himself surrounded with armed enemies, in a country of which he personated the legal monarch, and threatened with instant assassination—there was no possibility of avoiding extremities, no means of annihilating the treason, but by crushing the traitor:—no alternative, but by exemplary punishment, to avenge the *rights of insulted sovereignty*, or gallantly to perish in the unequal contest. It is a stigma on the Councils of the Company, on the politics of our Government, and on national justice, that it should have been possible, upon any resolutions formed here at home, upon any correspondence circulated abroad, or upon any instruction, hint, or insinuation from any interested person whatever, for the Governor-General to entertain the most distant suspicion of the probability of Rajah Cheyt Sing's restoration. Humanity, as well as policy, revolt

at

at the very idea. You, Sir, will join with me in pronouncing it a moral impoffibility.

Having toiled through 16 pages of Your Supplement to the fecond Report, in the doubly unpromifing attempt of demonftrating the criminality of Mr. Haftings, and the injured innocence of Cheyt Sing, You exhibit in the 20th page, all the melancholy fufferings of this " opprefled and unhappy man," under one point of view. It is, I confefs, a grand difplay of the pathetic, equally admirable for affecting tendernefs of language, and copious flow of invention: Worked up in a circumftantial climax of woe, each article gains more and more upon the commiferation of the reader, and each paufe affords a frefh opportunity for the effufion of fentiment. But that fhortnefs of fentence, which in fo mafterly a manner favours the burft of paffion, is no lefs adapted to the perfpecuity of inveftigation, and the convenience of reply. I fhall therefore take the liberty to divide the influence of thefe bewitching periods, by an unaffected, unfeeling comment upon each; and it cannot but prove a fatisfaction to You to reflect, that how much

foever

foever I may detract from the authenticity of the fubject, I fhall add in the fame degree to the merit of the *romance*. " An event," you fay, " fo extraordinary in itfelf, and of fo " much confequence, not only to the fuffer- " ing party, but to every Tributary to the " Company whatever may be his rank or fta- " tion, induced your Committee to invefti- " gate the fubject with precifion.—From *this* " *inveſtigation*" (of which I have already given ample fpecimens) " the following conclu- " fions may be drawn:"

" If the confideration of *public fervices* per- " formed to our nation by the father, is re- " quited by a violation of public faith to the " fon, upon pretences the moft frivolous"—

Comment. Bulwant Sing had not many *public fervices* to plead : and I am aftonifhed how the Prefident and Council of Bengal, in 1773, fhould allude to any *fervices* of the kind performed in 1764 (2d Report, page 11) when, *in that very year*, in the war with Sujah Dowla, his conduct betrayed fo much dupli- city, that the then Government wifhed to have him " *difpoffeffed of his Country, and his*

F

perfon,

" *perfon, if poffible, fecured.*" (page 5.) In 1765, 'he eloped from our army, and the letter from the Council, April 1, (page 9) is expreſſive of the ſtrongeſt diſtruſt, and complains of his " actual *violation of his treaty,*" by deſerting our arms. Our Government was even obliged to relinquiſh in his favour a conſiderable unli-quidated demand, " *in hopes of making it his* " *intereſt to remain faithful.*" The public ſer-vices performed by the father, and the viola-lation of public faith to the fon, are equally viſionary.— See Mr. Haſtings's excellent let-ter, (page 29, 30 and 31).

" If the ſolemn faith of a treaty, which " confirmed the Tributary in the actual poſ-" ſeſſion of his lands, be no longer conſidered " of ſufficient validity to protect him from " oppreſſion and extortion"——

Comment. I think I have clearly ſhewn that Cheyt Sing was *not exempted from military ſervice,* by the tenure of his Zemindarry: fo long therefore as the demands of Government, for the war eſtabliſhment, did not exceed the extent of his common military force, there was no oppreſſion or extortion in the cafe. The
Committee

Committee obferve (fupplement, page 19)
" that if there was *no boundary of* right, on
" which the Rajah could make his ftand to
" the increafing demands of the Governor-
" General and Council, he could not be faid to
" poffefs any right or property whatfoever."
I anfwer—that there *was* a boundary: that
the number of his troops in actual pay, or an
equivalent to that number, was the precife
boundary in queftion: and that whereas
Cheyt Sing's regular eftablifhment is ftated to
have been 7690 men (page 19) the Governor-General was much within the limits of
right, when he peremptorily demanded 3 battalions of feapoys, and 1000 cavalry.——A
requifition of this nature by no means inter-
fered with the ftipulations of the Pottah and
Sunnud.

" If the juft, regular and punctual performance of all ftipulated conditions, is found
to be no fecurity againft new claims and new
exactions"——

Comment. Colonel Monfon in his minute
refpecting the Governor-General's propofition
for engaging Cheyt Sing to maintain 2000 cavalry

valry (fupplement, page 12) thus exprefles himfelf. " I am of opinion, the Company " fhould receive the Rajah's *affiftance* on the " fame terms he *gave* it to the Vizier, or the " prefent Nabob."— General Clavering ftates, that 500 of his cavalry actually " *affifted* un- " der the command of the Captain of the " Governor's guard, on the conqueft of the " Rohilla Country."—The fovereignty of Benares was yielded to us by the Vizier, " with all the powers and rights annexed to " it," precifely as he had holden it : and the Committee now difpute our right to demand of Cheyt Sing *any affiftance at all.*

" If a Tributary of the Company is found " to have no other fecurity for the poffeffion " of his lands, *which defcended to him from ma-* " *ny generations,* but the arbitrary power of the " Governor-General, or executive Govern- " ment of the Country"———.

Comment. *Who* and *what* was Rajah Bul- want Sing's *father,* and where can it be found that Cheyt Sing came to the poffeffion of his lands *by defcent?* —The contrary is on proof above. Even had the Zemindarry been *bere-* *ditary,*

ditary, which, till fettled by Mr. Haftings in 1773, moft certainly was not the cafe ftill it muft have been held upon feodal principles, and the general laws of the Mogul empire. Military fervice is *military fervice*, and not the *arbitrary will of the Governor-General*. The pof-feffion of the land carried inherently with it that precife obligation, and its performance was a pledge for the fecurity of that pof-feffion.

" If the poffeffion of wealth is to be confi-
" dered as a ftate-crime, and heavy fines and
" penalties are to be laid on the poffeffors,
" with a view of rendering their power or
" their wealth lefs dangerous to the Com-
" pany"——

Comment. This is a jefuitical inference from a partial ftatement of a paragraph in the Governor-General's narrative. After explain-ing the grounds on which Cheyt Sing owed obedience to the Company, and reciting the different acts of contumacy, by which he had forfeited that obedience, he proceeds to fhew by what means he would extract *good* out of *evil*, and make the very punifhment of his
delin-

delinquency fubfervient both to the fafety and profit of the ftate. " I left Calcutta," fays he, (narrative, page 12) " impreffed with " the belief that extraordinary means were " neceffary, and thofe exerted with a ftrong " hand, to preferve the Company's interefts " from finking under the accumulated weight " which oppreffed them. I faw a *political ne-* " *ceffity* for curbing the *overgrown power* of a " great Member of their dominion, and mak- " ing it contribute to the relief of their pref- " ing exigencies."—If Cheyt Sing were pow- erful enough to difpute his Sovereign's au- thority in *one inftance*, (and that too upon unjuftifiable excufes, and contrary to the very tenure by which he enjoyed his territory) he might foon have become equally refractory or dilatory in the payment of his ftipulated rents—or have affumed any other undue pre- tenfion: and hence the neceffity for curbing his overgrown power, degenerated into info- lence. If his niggard obftinacy and fhamelefs prevarications had defrauded his paramount of a *timely aid*, which it was his duty, as a *Ze- mindar* to have furnifh'd, no won er that the damages accruing from fuch default were laid to his account, or that he were compelled to

contribute

contribute a larger portion of relief to thofe
preffing exigencies, which his undutiful conduct had fo much combined to aggravate.——
It was not the " *poffeffion of wealth*," that was
" *confidered as a ftate crime*," but a pertina-
cious reluctance to pay the juft demands of
Government; and if he relied on his wealth
or power as fufficient to fcreen him from the
juftice of his Sovereign—he from that moment muft be deemed a difaffected fubject, his
power and wealth were really dangerous, and
it became equally prudent, juft, and neceffary
to check them.

    " If the compliance with one arbitrary and
" unjuft demand, inftead of fecuring the tri-
" butary from further oppreffion, is inftantly
" followed by another demand fo extravagant,
" as to render a compliance with it utterly
" impoffible"——

Comment. Falfe throughout.—The firft
demand was neither *arbitrary* nor *unjuft*. I
have proved it to be *legal* and *conftitutional*;
nor can a *forced fubmiffion* to fuperior power be
ftrictly termed " *compliance*." The fecond demand fo far from being *impoffible*, was the very
reverfe

reverfe even of *extravagant*. It relates to the
requifition for cavalry: and it is proved by
Cheyt Sing's own confeffion, that he kept
1300 at leaft "The number required," fays
the Governor-General in the 7th page of his
narrative, "was 2000, and afterwards reduced
"to the demand of 1500, *and laftly to* 1000,
"but with no more fuccefs. *He offered* 250,
"*but furnifhed none.*"

"If requifitions are made, unauthorized
"by any ftipulation in the treaty, and a
"fhort delay intervenes before the requifi-
"tion is finally complied with, if fuch de-
"lay is conftrued into evidence of high
"treafon'———

Comment. The *requifitions* were made in
the fpirit of a *feodal obligation*, and the *ftipu-*
lations of the treaty had nothing to do with
them. *Would a crown-leafe in England abfolve*
me from allegiance to his Majefty, or taxes to the
State? The "*fhort delay*" before compliance is proved to have been of feveral
months in each year, and that upon pleas
equally indecent and untrue. After all, the
delay was never conftrued into *evidence of*
high

high treason, but treated for what it really was, *contumacy and disobedience*. When other *overt acts* had clearly established the *guilt of high treason*, the delay in complying with the demands of Government became one link in the grand chain of *evidence*, that clearly demonstrated *the previous existence of treasonable intentions*.

" If Reports unwarranted, and ill-authen-
" ticated,—if suggestions of public danger
" and imputations of evil designs, ill-found-
" ed, improbable and impracticable are to
" be admitted as sufficient grounds for com-
" mencing hostilities"——

Comment. W o commenced those hostili-
ties?—Cheyt Sing. No *evil designs* were *imputed*, till the country was in *actual revolt:* No *public dangers* were *suggested*, till two Com-panies of Seapoys had been *massacred in cold blood*. These are *facts*, certainly not *ill found-ed*, though they might be thought *improbable:* and *after perpetration* it is rather a bold figure of rhetoric to term them " *impracticable* " The " *Reports*" alluded to, were not be-lieved, at least no act was performed in con-

G   sequence

fequence of fuch belief, till *after conviction.*
But *Reports*, which upon after-difcovery are
found perfectly to tally with matter of fact,
and of which *upwards of fifty affidavits* teftify
the veracity, can never be deemed " *unwar-*
" *ranted or ill-authenticated.*"

" If the diftrefs of the Eaft-India Com-
" pany, from whatfoever caufe arifing,
" fhould ever be confidered as the fmalleft
" juftification of meafures, which are cruel,
" unjuft, and oppreffive to the natives of
" India"———.

Comment. A mere *petitio principii!* amplified with the cuftomary tautology of inappli-
cable epithets.—The diftrefs of the Eaft India
Company flattered Cheyt Sing with the
hopes of exerting his contumcy and difobedience unpunifhed; and his mifconduct
was a juftification for the Governor-General's
intended fine. His fubfequent efcape from
arreft, his maffacre of our troops, and open
rebellion, were a moft palpable *forfeiture* of
his *allegiance*, AND CONSEQUENTLY OF HIS
ZEMINDARRY.

" If

" If thefe conclufions be juft and well
" founded"——

Comment. They moft affuredly *are not* in
any one inftance, and therefore all farther
notice of them is nugatory and abfurd. But
if fuch glaring mifreprefentations are to pafs
for faƐt; if fuch odious partiality is to ftand
in the place of juftice; and if the legiflature,
the Government, and the Company are to be
deceived and mifled by fuch jefuitical artifices,
" *no fituation can be more wretched and deplo-*
" *rable,*" than that of men, who in great and
refponfible offices have performed the moft
glorious and important fervices to their
country, " *whofe honour, lives and fortunes*"
are expofed to the inveterate prejudices, the
felf-interefted machinations, and exaggerat-
ing narratives of a SeleƐt Committee !——

. I had intended, Sir, in this place to clofe
my obfervations on your curious Supplement
to the 2d Report.--But no fooner have I
fairly combated and completely overthrown
all Your unfupported affertions upon matter
of faƐt, than I a) peftered with fpeculative
abfurdities.

abfurdities. Who would have expected to find a man of Your political experience, vindicating the *uniformity* of the line of advancement in our Indian Governments? yet You boldly advance (Supplement, page 18) " this *regular and eftablifhed mode of fucceffion* " *to power*, fo frequently confirmed by practice, " when oppofed to the *great uncertainty* of " fucceffion among the Princes of India, has " been a matter of admiration to the natives " of Hindoftan." I am as great a friend as You can be to a regular and uniform fyftem of fucceffion, but for my foul I cannot difcover wherein the fucceffion to the Chair of Calcutta can appear *lefs uncertain to the natives of India*, than the fucceffion to the throne of Dehli! Did *no competition* arife concerning the fucceffion, upon the unwarrantable pretext of Mr. Haftings's refignation? Did no unexpected revolution ever take place in Fort St. George, " dependant neither on " *beredita y right, priority of birth, the appoint-* " *ment of the late profeffor, the election of the* " *people*, nor any other *fixed* or *determinate* " *rule?*"—Surely, Sir, You compofed this paragraph in a very abfent ftate of mind,— pondering, perhaps upon the fingularity of the

the revolution, by which Meffrs. Powel and Bembridge had *fucceeded* again to *their* offices!— Alas, alas! the people of India well know, that there are other myfteries in the world, befides " *the intrigues of the Seraglio :*" and that if an old woman from the inmoft receffes of her Zennana can foment a rebellion in Oude, a patriot and legiflator can impofe upon the fenfes, and warp the judgement of half a nation for two years together, by interefted, " *ill-founded,*" and " *ill-authenti-* " *cated*" rhapfodies from a Committee Chamber.

The mention of the Seraglio naturally leads me to the fubject of your 10th Report— much more naturally than an appointment to take into confideration the ftate of the adminiftration of juftice in the provinces of Bengal, Bahar, and Oriffa, could lead You to fcrutinize the internal politics of the kingdom of Oude. But this circumftance ferves to give You a more exclufive title to the compofition before us, as your magnificent Chairman, with all his front, is no Hibernian.—This is the fourth Report which has already grown out of the Governor General's

late

late journey to Benares and Oude ; and I do not doubt but that from the very fame mate-rials, and with equal attention to facts, the Committee, if permitted, would contrive to fabricate half a dozen more Reports for the next feffions, all " *confidered as their indifpenfa-* " *ble duty.*" " An inveftigation into the " *caufes affigned by the Governor-General,* for a " breach of the public faith of the Company, " pledged by him and the Council-General, " in the moft folemn manner, for the protec-" tion of the widow of the late Vizier Sujah " Dowla, a woman of the firft diftinction, " by birth and rank, in the empire of Hin-" doftan," is the oftenfible purport of your performance, and the poor helplefs lady has found in You a moft zealous and hardy ad-vocate.

This lady, who is known by the denomination of the *Bow Begum,* advanced in the year 1775, a fum of money *to her fon* the Vizier, to be applied to the exigences of the ftate, " on con-" dition that fhe fhould be guaranteed by the " Company in the full and quiet enjoyment " of *her* eftates, effects, and jagheers." (10th Report, page 4.) The public faith being accordingly

accordingly pledged to the *mother* of the Vizier, fhe continued to refide, under that protection, at Fyzabad. " Not indeed in the
" unmolefted enjoyment of *her* rights ; for
" your *Committee obferve*, (page 4) that fo early
" as January, 1778, the Englifh Refident,
" Mr. Middleton, makes very ftrong repre-
" fentations to the Governor-General and
" Council, of the Vizier's treatment of his
" *grandmother*." No other Member of the
Committee, Sir, can have any pretenfions to
this very conclufive *obfervation :* The *fyllogifm*
effectually befpeaks its *author*. After the
death of the Vizier Sujah Dowla, his widow,
the Bow Begum, unwarrantably poffeffed herfelf of his effects. Our Refident at Oude
writes (Appendix, No. 1.) "I underftand the
" late Vizier depofited the *furplus of his reve-*
" *nues* with the Begum ; and having died in-
" teftate (or at leaft a will was never pro-
" duced, *though one is faid to be fecreted by the*
" *Begum)* it left a door open to the difputes
" which have happened ; for *according to the*
" *Koran*, and the *ufages of the country*, the Na-
" bob could *claim an infinitely greater fhare*
" than he has got." In another place he
mentions to have infinuated to the Begum herfelf

felf (Appendix, No. 1,) "That the treafures
"fhe poffeffed were *the treafures of the ftate*, as
"fhe had not fucceed d to them by any *legal*
"*right*, and they had been hoarded up *to pre-*
"*vide againft an emergency.*" Here we have a
woman *fufpected to have fecreted her hufband's*
will, and notorioufly affuming to her private
ufe *treafures deftined for the exigencies of the ftate.*
Her fon, however, in a moment of diftrefs,
was content to relinquifh all *his legal right* in
thofe treafures, for a very fcanty portion of
their amount. At this time, as well as at all
fubfequent periods, the Old Lady feems to
have behaved with peculiar acrimony towards
him, for the Council-General, on the conclu-
fion of this tranfaction, thus write to their
Refident, at Oude, (Appendix, No. 1) "We
"think that the circumftances of the Nabob's
"affairs, and *the unfavourable difpofition which*
"*his mother, the Begum, fhewed towards him,*
"made it neceffary for you to comply with
"his requeft, for affording *your affiftance to*
"*perfuade her* to fupply him with a fum of
"money." The Begum indeed had roundly
told the Refident, that "as for the Nabob,
"*fhe would not advance him a fingle rupee* upon
"his own word, but fooner throw all her
                                        "jewels,

" jewels and money into the river."—And he
writes, " that the Begum claimed every arti-
" cle of the late Vizier's property, *even to his*
" *military stores* :" and he bears teftimony alfo
to the very improper conduct of the Begum's
fervants, " who have hitherto preferved a to-
" tal independence of the Nabob's authority,
" *beat the officers of his Government*, and refufed
" obedience to his Perwannahs." The language of this " helplefs woman" appears on
all occafions, fturdy and affuming.—In one
letter fhe requefts the Governor-General to
difplace the Nabob's Minifter, and put her
confidants in his place; and that " whatever
" fums are due to the Englifh Chiefs," *fhe*
" *will caufe to be paid out of the Revenues.*"
In another fhe writes to the Refident, " You
" were a party in this affair, and took from
" me the fum of 56 lacks of rupees. If you
" will caufe the 56 lacks to be reftored to me,
" then the Coulnama will not be binding:
" and do not you then take any part in the
" affair, and then let Afoph úl Dowla and
" Murteza Khan," (i. e. the Nabob and his
minifter) " *in whatever manner they are able,*
" take fums of money from *me, they will*
" *then fee the confequences.*" The Nabob him-

felf declared to the Resident his own opinion of his mother's ambitious views, by observing that " *Two rulers were too much for one country.*" Her language and Her conduct, as above described, do not *authorize*, they *palliate* at least, those severities which the Vizier is said to have exercised towards his mother, and which seem to have required the constant interference of our Resident to mollify. The general disposition however of both parties towards each other, is plainly deducible from their mutual recriminations, and mutual distrust. The Begum appears a " capricious, " inconstant, violent" woman, ambitious of acquiring, "*by the intrigues of the seraglio,*" management of all the revenues of the country. Possessed of immense treasures by a suspected fraudulent concealment of her husband's will, at best by a very dubious title, and *against the usages of her religion and country,* she " presumes to talk of appointing mini-" sters, and governing kingdoms."—The Nabob is, by his mother, represented as a man " entirely inexperienced in the affairs of the " world, and ignorant of what is good or " bad," and by the Resident, as having " so " entirely lost the confidence and affections of

"his

" his fubjects, that unlefs fcme reftraint is im-
" pofed upon him, which would effectually fe-
" cure thofe who live under the protection of his
" Government, from violence and oppreffion ;"
no man of reputation or property would long
continue to inhabit his dominions. Such were
the inclinations, and fuch the behaviour of the
two parties in 1776 ; the Refident then wrote,
" I find all my endeavours to reconcile her
" (the Begum) and the Nabob in vain:" and
in another place " I have hitherto been un-
" able to fatisfy the Nabob or the Begum.—
however, a fpecious formal kind of agreement
was then patched up between them, to which
the Refident was guarantee : But it cannot be
faid to have been very fatisfactory on either
fide, as the Nabob could get but *a part of*
what the Refident thought him fully entitled
to demand, and even of that part it appeared,
" by the behaviour of the Begum's Eunuchs
" and fervants, that they were inclined to pro-
" craftinate the payment upon any frivolous
" pretence that occured." The difputes which
the Refident's interpofition had lulled in 1776,
broke out with frefh violence in 1798. And
as far as appears upon the Committee's ftatement of the cafe, there is *reafon* to fuppofe

that

that the Council-General's authority with the Vizier, at that time, *silenced* at leaſt, if it could not aſſuage His diſcontents. But there is *no reaſon*, either from any actual documents in the Report and Appendix, or from analogical conjecture and compariſon, to preſume, that the Begum's temper had abated any thing of its former violence, and her ambition of its pretenſions ; or that if her ſervants had " pre- " ſerved a total independence of the Nabob's " authority, beat the officers of his govern- " ment, and *refuſed obedience to his Perwan- " nabs*," in 1776, when ſhe was really " *a* " *helpleſs woman*," at the abſolute power and diſpoſal of a deſpotic ſovereign, her conduct ſhould have become more moderate, or that of her ſervants more obſequious afterwards, when ſhe flattered herſelf with an utter ex- emption from all controul, by virtue of the Company's guarantee.

In 1781, " The Province of Oude, having " fallen into a ſtate of great diſorder and " confuſion, its reſources being in an ex- " traordinary degree diminiſhed, and the " Nabob Aſoph ul Dowla, having earneſtly " entreated the preſence of the Governor-.
" General,

" General, and declared, that unlefs fome
" effectual meafures are taken for his relief,
" he muft be under the neceffity of leaving
"-his country, and coming down to Calcutta
" to reprefent his fituation," it was refolved
in Council, that the Governor-General fhould
vifit that Province, and ufe his endeavours
for the re-eftablifhment of its affairs. Benares lay in his way, and having much reafon
to be diffatisfied with Rajah Cheyt Sing, he
took that opportunity to bring him to order.
The unhappy confequences that followed,
have been already explained. Cheyt Sing
refifted his authority, fled from arreft, murdered his guards, and commenced open rebellion, " Its contagion," Mr. Haftings ob-
ferves in his narrative (page 26) " inftantly
" flew to Fyzabad,"—which the Nabob
Vizier, in expectation of the Governor-
General's vifit had already quitted. The
revolt at Benares commenced on the 16th of
Auguft, and about the 8th of September,
the commotions are faid to have begun in
Oude. The firft interview between the Governor-General and the Nabob Vizier, was on
the 11th of September, at Chunar Gur: at
which time it was not probable that either

party

party fhould have received intelligence of the difturbances at Fyzabad, and therefore the Governor-General, in his letter to Mr. Wheler of that date (10th Report, page 9) confines his account to the rebellion in Gauzipoor: There is no document whatever *to prove,* that even at that moment Mr. Haftings had entertained the moft diftant idea of giving up the Company's Guarantee, which fecured to the two Begums the poffeffion of their Jagheers, much lefs that when he left Calcutta, fuch a defign had ever once occurred to him.—But when he wrote a fecond time on the 18th of September to Mr. Wheler, He informed him, that the contagion had reached the Province of Oude, but that He " fhould difmifs the Nabob in a few days, " and doubted not but his troubles would " foon be quelled." The next day being the 19th of September, the Governor-General, and the Nabob Vizier mutually exchanged certain articles of agreement, which had been concerted between them as the moft probable means for reftoring the Province of Oude " to its former ftate of affluence, good " order, and profperity." From a review of thefe dates, it is clear to demonftration, that

accounts

accounts of the infurrection at Fyzabad had
reached Mr. Haftings, between the 11th and
18th of September: and it may be fairly in-
ferred, that He and the Nabob agreed in
confidering "the military power and do-
"minion affumed by the Jagheerdars" to
have afforded at once the temptation and the
means for rebellion. It was therefore fettled
between them, that the Nabob fhould be
" permitted to refume fuch as he might find
" neceffary," with a referve that he fhould
pay the nett amount of the collections of
fuch as were guaranteed by the Company.—
At the head of the Jagheerdars were the two
Begums: and to thofe who fhall have obferved the uniform ambition, violent temper,
and habitual difobedience of thofe ladies,
their eunuchs and fervants, as defcribed in the
16th Report, and who fhall have perufed
the feveral affidavits in the Appendix, No. 3,
to the Governor-General's Narrative, namely
of Doord Sing L; of Ahlaud Sing M; of
Denoo Sing N; of Ram Sing O; of Hur-
deal Sing P; and of Bejy Sing Q; befides
thofe of the Refident, of Lieutenant Colonel
Hannay, and other European witneffes, who
all fwear either to the general difaffection of
the

the Begums, or to particular and pointed
acts of treachery and revolt, perpetrated at
their inftigation, and *in their name*, it will not
be poffible to doubt, that the Governor-General and the Nabob acted upon full conviction of their delinquency, in the prefent
inftance, as well as of their having " in-
" variably employed the *influence* of their
" Jagheers to the moft pernicious purpofes."
When thefe articles were drawn up, Mr.
Haftings appears to have had no other view,
than to ftrengthen the Nabob's hands by a
political fuppreffion of that delegated authority, which was rifing faft into independence
and to increafe his revenues by the fums in
which the actual produce of the Jagheers
fhould be found to exceed the nominal value
of the grant. The Nabob, as a Sovereign,
could not but wifh fuch an addition to his
own power, and the actual ftate of his country muft have impreffed him with an idea of
its neceffity. No wonder therefore, that
upon his return to his capital, " the Go-
" vernor-General fhould expect that he would
" immediately have entered into the execu-
" tion of the meafures neceffary for the ac-
" complifhment of the plan they had mu-
" tually

" tually agreed upon, and *particularly the re-*
" *fumption of the Jagheers*, as an act equally
" neceffary to the reftoration of peace, and
" to the difcharge of his debts to the Com-
" pany." Imbecility and irrefolution were
however the characteriftics of the Nabob's
Councils, and it appears that the month of
December arrived without any progrefs having been made in the bufinefs. But the
harfhnefs of the Nabob towards the Begums,
from the firft moment of his acceffion to the
mufnud (which I have above defcribed from
your 10th Report) added to his recent experience of their intrigues, leave no room to
fuppofe with You, (page 11) that " this
" temporizing and indecifive conduct" could
proceed from any tendernefs he entertained
for his parents. True it is, the Governor-
General was alarmed, and with reafon, at the
delay. To have returned to Calcutta, leaving one grand end of his journey under an
apparent improbability of completion, would
have diftreffed a man lefs warm than himfelf for the intereft of his employers. He
therefore pointedly haftened its accomplifh-
ment, by the ftrong interference of the Refi-

I   dent.

dent. This was in the latter end of December, 1781.

At this period a new scene opens.—We have seen the Bow Begum openly countenancing an infurrection in the heart of her fon's dominions, in September, 1781, and we have seen the Nabob entering into a fpecific agreement for depriving her of that undue influence which fhe derived from her jagheer, but allowing her the nett amount of its produce, About the latter end of September Afoph ul Dowla returned to his capital, at the earneft inftances of the Governor-General, and for the exprefs purpofe of reforming the overgrown jagheers. At the fame time our Refident at the Vizier's court received inftructions from Mr. Haftings, to attend to the due execution of the articles of agreement juft concluded. Some time in December the Refident informed the Governor-General, that the Nabob had fhewn a great reluctance to enter on this bufinefs, but that he had at length appointed an Aumil to take charge of the Begum's jagheer. You are pleafed to obferve, Sir, (10th Report, page 20) that " the refumption of the jag-
" heers was an act *totally unneceffary* to the re-
" ftoration

" ftoration of the peace of the country, be-
" caufe *that peace* had been reftored before the
" refumption was made." The country, I
grant, had affumed the *appearance* of peace.—
The revolters *refted on their arms.* It was effectually *to fecure* future tranquillity, to de-
prive intrigue of its *refources*, and rebellion of
its *fupport*, that the refumption of the jagheers
was propofed. The clans in Scotland were
abolifhed, not to procure prefent quiet, but to
obviate the poffibility of future difturbance.
Events amply juftified the Governor-General's
impatience, and evinced the prudence, the
policy, the neceffity of this refumption. For
although it be ftated, " that the return of
" the Nabob had *effectually* reftored the quiet
" of the country."—Yet we find that the inftant he proceeded to act upon the articles
ftipulated between Mr Haftings and himfelf,
the ftandard of revolt was again fet up, and
" *the Begum affembled a large body of troops*," (in
her fon's capital) with a fuppofed defign of
refiftance. " A violent and threatening letter
" which" the Refident writes to " have juft
" received from the Begum, would feem to
" leave no room to doubt of her intentions to
" fupport *the already declared licentioufnefs of*

" *her*

" *her servants, in opposing the Nabob's orders.*" It appears, (10th Report, page 10) that the Nabob's Aumil for taking charge of the Begum's jagheers, was appointed *before the 19th of December*; and it was on *the 12th of January* following, that the Resident, in conjunction with the Nabob, found it necessary to assume them by force of arms. Averse to every species of subordination, and emboldened perhaps by former impunity, the two leading Eunuchs of this turbulent and imperious woman had exerted themselves during the whole of that interval, in assembling, and calling in armed men from all quarters : (Appendix, No. 6.) They had even fortified and entrenched themselves with a view to resistance, in the Begum's Kellah (or Castle.) And when they at last submitted to superior force, were found possessed of a very large store of ammunition, properly distributed—" *drawn up in regular order,* " *pieces loaded, and matches lighted.*" Such clear proofs of premeditated opposition to the commands of *their* Sovereign, *absolute* at all events with respect to *them,* and in *whom* (even if we admit the Begum herself to have had an independent right to her jagheer) *resistance* was certainly *rebellion,* and the preparations for

resistance

refiftance *treafon*, cannot be overturned by any
fophiftical diftinctions and prevaricating quib-
bles of a Select Committee. Nor could the
confequences of this frefh provocation be other
than we find in the Report, *a feizure of the Begum's ill-gotten and ill-applied treafures.* This
brings me, Sir, to your grand mafter-piece of
infinuation, to your laboured attempts to infer,
that Mr. Haftings has facrificed every moral
obligation, and every tie of national honour, to
the mere temporary advantage of his employers. Having ftated the failure of the expected
relief from Cheyt Sing's wealth, and quoted
the Governor-General's declaration, " that
" the Company's interefts could only be pre-
" ferved from finking under the accumulated
" weight which oppreffed them, by the ex-
" ertion, with a ftrong hand, of fome extra-
" ordinary means." You pointedly and tri-
umphantly exclaim, " *he appears to have fe-
" lected a new object for this exertion."* No doubt
t had been one great motive of Mr. Haftings's journey to Oude, to recover, (and
with juftice) as much as poffible of the enor-
mous balance in which the Vizier ftood en-
gaged to the Company ; as well as to alleviate

by

by an immediate fine on Cheyt Sing, the pecuniary diftreffes of the moment.—The two
objects were perfectly diftinct ; and if in the
one cafe the Governor-General has imparted
to us his own fecret of the intended mulct, in
the other he has uniformly maintained, that
he looked to a reform in the finances of Oude,
for the means of a gradual extinction of the
Vizier's debts.—With this profeffed determi-
nation he left Calcutta; upon thefe grounds he
concerted his plan with the Vizier, and to thefe
arrangements he confined his expectations for
the Company's relief; in order to convict him
of having " felected a new object" *per fas et
nefas,* immediately upon and in confequence
of his difappointment with refpect to Cheyt
Sing, it is incumbent on you to prove, deci-
fively, *pofitively,* and incontrovertibly, that
he not only propofed, but abfolutely deter-
mined and concluded an agreement to this
purpofe with the Vizier, *viva voce,* at Chunar :
and that the feizure of the Begum's wealth
would and *muft* have taken place, even had
fhe quietly, obediently, and with a good grace,
given up charge of her jagheers on the firft
requifition of the Nabob's Aumil. Every fen-

tence

tence of your report proves by inference the direct contrary. No mention whatever, no hint, no fufpicion of fuch an intention tranf-pires, till the 13th of January, 1782, and then no more than a furmife. It bears no part whatever in the inftructions from the Gover-nor-General to the Refident ; it is not alluded to in the agreements between him and the Vizier; and on the very 13th of January, when the Refident informs Mr. Haftings of his having been obliged, by force of arms, to put the Nabob's party in poffeffion of the Begum's fortrefs, he appears totally unap-prized of any defign in either party, to appro-priate her treafures to public ufes. The firft opening of the bufinefs comes in communi-cation from the Nabob himfelf, and the very expreffion of his letter bears teftimony to its being an *after-thought*, and an expedient *very lately devifed.* " I have" fays he, " to confirm " and increafe our friendfhip, even done that " which was *not thought of, or refolved.*" (10th. Report, page 12.) This was alfo on the 13th of January. The Governor-General, in his letter of the 23d of January, mentions, for the firft time that " in addition to the former refolution " of refuming the Begum's jagheers, theNabob " had

" had declared his refolution of reclaiming all
" the treafures of his family which were in
" their poffeffion." (Appendix, No. 6.) If
thefe two refolutions had been co-exiftent, that
for refuming the jagheers could not have been
the " *former.*" If the circumftance had been
mentioned to the Nabob at the time of draw-
ing up the articles of agreement in September,
1781, he would not have written in January,
1782, that he had done that which was *not
thought of*; and how much foever your Committee may perceive, by a perufal of the
Vizier's letters, " the abfolute dependence of
his fituation," (Page 21) *this* of the 13th of
January is beyond a doubt, both in ftile and
fubject, *exclufively his own.* Mr. Haftings, in
this letter of the 23d January, mentions, that
he had " ftrenuoufly encouraged and fupported
" the Vizier" in the refolution of affuming
his mother's treafures, and founds his advice
on experience of the pernicious ufes to which
they had been hitherto perverted. *Then* it is
alfo, that we have the firft intimation of a defign to apply this wealth to the liquidation of
the Company's demands. Mr. Haftings had
been originally fatisfied with the hopes of a
gradual but regular difcharge.—The new turn
of

of events, the incorrigible obſtinacy of the Begum, and the juſt provocations given to the Nabob, preſented him a brighter proſpect; and by a wonderful co-incidence of fortunate occurrences with his own ſtrenuous exertions, he was enabled to recover the whole of that debt *at once*, and within *two months* of the pre-ciſe date of Mr. Francis's moſt exhilarating epiſtle, which aſſured the Directors, " that " this debt, ſo far from being diſcharged, " is by this time immoderately increaſed, " and never can be diſcharged out of the " revenues of Oude." (Appendix to the 2d Report, No. 7.) How much foever the Nabob had reſolved to do that which was *not thought of*, and how much foever the Governor-General had encouraged him in his reſolutions, no trace is to be found of the mode by which the ſentiments of each party upon this head were communicated. We can therefore only judge that it muſt have been thro' the medium of ſome Vackeel, or confidential Miniſter, and moſt probably between the 19th of December, when it was known that the Nabob's Aumil had been repulſed in his attempt to take charge of the Begum's jag-

K   heer,

heer, and the 12th of January, when the Nabob's troops entered her Kellah. Yet *even they*, after such a series of disobedience, treason, and revolt, no very harsh or violent measures seem to have been pursued with the old lady. The Resident writes on the 3d of Feb. " that in his letters of the 20th, 25th, and " 27th ultimo, he had mentioned that the " Bow Begum had finally *agreed to deliver up* " the treasures of the late Nabob." —*Therefore* they were *not forced* from her in the moment of victory, and in the ardour of rapacity. An interval of at least 12 days, by the Committee's own account, (page 13) passed before she agreed to surrender her wealth ; and in that period we can but suppose parleys, proposals, and negociations to have taken place (though not yet come to hand) by which the Begum was at length induced —perhaps not with the best grace in the world—to *agree* to deliver up her treasures. If She *did agree*, (and You, Sir, have not been pleased to controvert *that* point) the original *treaty* between Her and her Son was *dissolved by consent*, and the Guarantee *became void of course*. Where then is this " breach " of

" of the public faith of the Company," ?
this bugbear of " a measure, which has ren-
" dered the English name odious and de-
" testable" to be found? — Only, Sir, in
Your heated imagination: in that repository
of unnatural conceits, pathetic extravagan-
cies, and incurable prejudices.

My letter has drawn to so unexpected a
length, that I shall not stay to refute in form.
Your tedious comments on the Governor-
General's acceptance of ten lacks of Rupees
from the Vizier. Mr. Haftings has thro' life
been so uniformly and so notoriously infen-
fible to pecuniary advantages, that I almost
wonder he should even now have troubled
himself to utter a wish on the subject. The
doctrine of presents, as a compliment of uni-
verfal use in Afia, is perfectly understood in
this Country. An act of Parliament pro-
hibits the Company's servants from the receipt of presents. But the fame act expresses
that any such present accepted, taken, or
received, shall be deemed to have been received for the fole use of the Company.—Be it
so.—Mr. Haftings accepted 10 lacks of ru-

pees,

pees, and in conformity to the act, appro-
priated them to the Company's service. But
as this sum was over and above all the dues,
debts, and demands of the Company on the
Vizier, the Governor-General hoped the
length, the importance, the integrity, and the
success of his services, might reasonably be
pleaded as a claim upon the deposit. He wishes
to owe his fortune to the bounty of his Employers, not to the civility of the Vizier;
and the validity of his pretensions will be
weighed in an assembly, where, believe me,
Sir, your credit will kick the beam.

I shall now take the liberty to close my
present correspondence with you, and I flatter
myself there will never more be occasion to
renew it. Your political taper has long since
stunk in the socket: Its flame, I think, expired in the whining letter to your enlight-
ened constituents of Bristol. If appearances may be trusted, your public existence
hangs on a very slender thread indeed; nor
do I think it possible that the Select Committee should fulminate through another
sessions.—But I may be mistaken. The minister

nifter of the day may find it *convenient* to keep You above ftairs. Should you, however, be again let loofe upon the Governor-General, my pen is ftill at your fervice. And though I fhall live to be afhamed of having wafted my time and trouble, in combating fuch unfubftantial fantoms, I take a pride in fubfcribing myfelf,

   Right Honourable Sir,

     Your determined Antagonift

      In the Caufe of Mr. Haftings,

        D E T E C T O R.

October 18, 1783.

www.ingramcontent.com/pod-product-compliance
Lightning Source LLC
Chambersburg PA
CBHW030004030726
47499CB00008B/2884